Sound Tapestry

by

Dawn Hartley

ISBN: 0-75965-579-0

This book is printed on acid free paper.

1stBooks – rev. 8/10/01

Poets

I shall try and tell you the composition of
A Poet, true and gifted artist of romanticism
and love.
Admittedly notorious to a fault
Rogues storing feelings like gold in a
secret vault.

The sky is simply not the sky.
A cloud is not something floating up high.
A rainbow not a simple band of different hues,
A state of depression simply not a case of blues!

A nearness to the fireplace not a search for warm.
A beautiful, raging, rain not a simple storm.
A love of chocolate ice cream not a childhood dream,
A cry of loneliness not a simple scream!

A day spent with a friend, not a wasteful time.
His warmth and laughter more precious than the
gift of rhyme.
These are all treasures locked in a special box,
A collection of sorts, like seashells, marbles,
or rocks!

A true love is never a casual affair.
But someone who risk his heart should he dare
Giving it freely yet knowing all the while
The one he gives it to is both woman and child!

For a poet lives not only in fantasy
But in the harsh reality
That this love could very well be
Her only link to true sanity!

A poet's thoughts roam at will.
One moment quiet, calm and still
The next chasing some falling star
Creating a dream distant and far!

Falling in love with a poet, a difficult game!
Because moment to moment, feelings never stay
the same.
Like a Knight on some Holy Crusade
A promise spoken truly a promise made!

Poet's hearts are not bound by man exclusively
But are guided by only the Deity!
God made their spirits of a special clay
Wet it with the ability to love, come what may!

Read these verses most carefully,
For hidden among them a special key
Giving this poet's heart to you for safe keeping,
And a bed far more wonderful than merely sleeping!

Silence

Do you not speak for fear of saying what you feel?
Or is it because what you feel is real.
Do you not love me for fear of receiving what you need so
much?
Or is it because you don't need someone warm to touch.

Is it lack of happiness that hides your smile?
Or is it you think they are out of style.
Do you not love me for fear of being caught?
Or is it the hurt lack of love has taught.

Do you pretend that I am not around
Because it's love you know you've found?
Or is it because you are hurt and blue
And need someone to just love you.

Specialty Parts

You love me with your eyes
Like clouds decorate blue skies.
You love me with your smile
With the honesty of a small child!

You love me with your heart
You're my best friend, daytime and dark.
But if you loved me with all of you,
I would be as high as the skies blue!

Reflections

There is a time in our lives, we would
all like to relive.
A time of loving, laughter, sharing more
than we had to give.
Someone tall, dark, and handsome,
maybe just medium and blond
Someone of whom you were very fond.

Your very own quarterback in the
neighborhood park.
That special warm and closeness
in the dark.
Chocolate ice cream all over your face
That big blue balloon you both chased!

That very, very, special friend
Whose life you never dreamed would end.
The unusual chill in the summer air
An unreal silence beyond compare.

But life goes on and times change
Things in your present to rearrange.
Yet always alive in your mind,
that unique time
When being in love had no reason or rhyme.

Hero's

I sat staring at the chess board
Suddenly they resembled G. Is
You, Viet Nam,
Half a world away!

Napalm falls on the enemy
And soaks like a summer rain.
Choppers hover like hornets
Some fly away but some stay behind!

I read letters and taste the fear.
Somewhere tonight in Viet Nam
The six o'clock media circus
Pictures for the folks back home!

Soldiers in boxes covered with flags.
Funerals on grassy hills
White crosses row after row
Classmates who won't laugh anymore!

I saw the soldiers come up the drive,
The doorbell rang, I tried not to hear.
"We regret to inform you"
The tears fell, suddenly I couldn't see.

I saw the coffin, our beautiful flag
The sun was shining but I felt a chill
I didn't hear the jets fly over head,
But the echo of rifle fire remains.

I remember another day
You pulled my hair on the merry-go-round.
I got up to run but had to look back
You tackled me and we rolled in the grass.
And I see your smile on your son's face.

Dawn Hartley

The Creation of a Firefighter

God took some very special clay
Made this man a most unique way.
He gave him softness of touch
And the ability to care so much.

He gave him no meaning for defeat,
And He gave him "Hell Fire" to beat.
He gave him warm, loving eyes,
Feelings for those times he cries.

He gave him a deep respect for his fellow man.
He gave him faith, hope, and ability to understand.
He personified the word, "Dedication"
In this "Firefighter", His best creation!

But most important, He gave him His love,
A divine gift from up above.
A guardian angel to guard his way.
A job in Heaven, painting rainbows after a rainy day.

Dracula Syndrome

Deep in the night, we leave home
And embark into the Dracula syndrome.
We go forth to serve those in need.
Unlike Dracula, who journeyed out to feed.

But dark holds many dangers.
Among these a multitude of strangers.
Headlights and street lights burning bright.
But not as warm as Dracula's sunlight.

All of us working for money to spend
Counting the hours until the darkness ends.
All of us on a nightly quest,
To serve and protect, to do our best.

We're deep in sleep during the day.
The rest of the world at work or play.
Deep nights weave a magic of a special kind.
And sunshine tends to make us blind.

So venture out into the dark, take a chance!
You could find Dracula, a man of romance.
Someone to bite your neck or hold you tight
To brighten your day and enchant your night!

Dawn Hartley

A Nurse by Definition

A Registered Nurse, a person with a degree
Special papers, something like a pedigree.
LVN, PRN, Vocational, titles earned
For medical information learned.

Look beyond those letters, passed that name
Feel the special warmth and caring
from an inward flame.
A desire to help those ever in need
Bound to that spirit, heart and deed.

More than a uniform, shots and pills
A friend to fight physical and emotional ills.
A hand to hold as death comes near
Reassurance to a child there's nothing to fear.

A warm secure welcome to a newborn baby
A touch of reality to a youth on a drug,
going crazy.
Someone to hug as death takes your best friend,
Someone whose job doesn't end.

Look deep into eyes that smile, sparkle and shine.
Listen to a voice concerned, sincere, and kind.
Here is the definition that you seek
A nurse is a person truly unique.

Someone to rebound your feelings when you
need to talk.
Someone to lean on when surgery makes it
difficult to walk.
Someone who knows the importance of
the human touch
Someone who knows tears can cure so much!

Someone whose job is not just eight hours long.
Who must be tender, yet always strong.
Someone who stores memories deep inside,
A Nurse is love personified!

Dawn Hartley

Love Written Down

Love is an emotion written down
Love on paper, absent of sound.
A poem is a thought not easily expressed.
But you could feel it if I were undressed.

Words are safe, though not so warm.
As being with you in an emotional storm.
I'm trying to protect you from my crazy mood.
I could easily remove your clothes, but that would be rude.

Know that I will take a dare!
Give me an address, I'll be there.
To listen, to love, to understand
The dreams and needs of a special man.

A Creature of Habit

Today a little sparrow sat quiet and shy
On a cold curb watching humanity pass by.
He had ruffled feathers against the cold
But the peace he enjoyed made him bold.

If we could make verbal his thoughts
He would probably recite all of man's faults.
For throughout history there has always been
The quiet, little sparrow and his kin.

As I sat watching this agile little bird
My mind reflected upon things I had heard.
Amid all the unhappiness, sadness, and unrest
This little, living creature faithfully builds his nest.

This tells me he has an inward source
That carefully plots his course.
Despite the problems man has to solve
He knows his difficulties will be resolved!

Thus, when he becomes bored by humanities pace,
He simply flies off to his sacred place.
Safe from man's destruction and pain
To enjoy in peace the tranquil rain.

Expectations of a Man In Blue

As a citizen, these are the things I expect of you.
To personify the meaning of an "Officer in Blue."
Dedication to the oath you have spoken
A willingness to serve that can't be broken.

That special ingredient that makes you unique.
A warmth and kindness when a citizen you meet.
The use of tact and decorum in word and deed,
The honor and pride that comes with a shield and creed.

Remember I don't care what the newspaper has to say.
Their job is to sensationalize in any way.
I want to know if my life was in danger
You would save me from the hands of a stranger.

I can only believe in the events that take place.
Trust the emotions I see on your face.
Yours is the voice I listen to,
I must know those words are honest and true.

These are but a few of my expectations.
I expect only the best of your judgment in all situations.
What is the most important way to show me you care?
When I need you, just please be there!

Undercover Moods

At work, a man always in disguise.
But I could always recognize those eyes.
A man in secret with a job to do.
Bet I could work undercover with you!

A man searching the city for vice
But a man whose vices are especially nice.
A man spending his nights making arrest
But a man whose love is the very best.

A special man with a shield and a gun
Fighting crime, staying on the run.
But a warm man in my bed at night
A man who holds me so close and tight!

A man away for too long at a time.
Putting his life on the line to stop crime,
But when he's home and safe at last,
I will love him till that time is passed!

Dawn Hartley

A Traffic Situation

Trapped alone in a dumb situation
Wonder why I drove passed the gas station?
The answer to my question wasn't far
Help at last, a police car.

I looked around for drivers I.D.
There you stood quietly looking at me.
You dwell in a world different from mine
Danger, fighting drugs and crime.

You were all business, soft-spoken, yet shy.
As I tried to explain and justify.
The problem was simple to resolve
But the reason for our meeting harder to solve.

You helped me out, I was on my way,
Silently wishing you a safe beautiful day.
We spent time lost in conversation
Trapped together in mutual fascination.

We talked about things that touch our lives,
Babies, hospitals, drunks, and knives.
I was visiting the brown of your eyes
When you caught me with quiet surprise.

You smiled at me yet I knew
You had found me and I found you.
You're my very, very special friend.
And the bond we share will never end.

I can tell you things that I feel
Anger, pain, loneliness, things that are real.
You share with me things touching you
Traffic, danger, domestics things that are true.

I treasure moments that we share
Because I know you really care
Sometimes together, yet apart
I never shared your body, but I touched your heart!!

Rescued

For a moment, I was in a safe place
Held very carefully in a warm embrace.
I heard your voice with words sincere
Their message to me quite clear!

You were the lighthouse, safety on the beach.
Guiding me from the angry ocean's reach.
The panic and anger couldn't withstand
The sanctuary of your outstretched hand!

A hug can mean so very much.
Friends have a very special touch.
Like a rainbow in a stormy sky,
Friends possess magic to make you fly!

Guardian Angels

Special people when they die
Must earn their wings so they can fly.
Angels assigned to be a guide
To watch, to protect, to walk along side.

I'm sure I have one for you see
Getting into mischief comes naturally for me.
Mine must be special indeed
Because I am a case always in need!

Sometimes I feel a tug on my arm
Trying to protect me from danger or harm.
My angel must be masculine for sure
Because I do things no female could endure.

But there are days I can tell
When my angel wishes I would behave well.
So that he could take a vacation
Instead of watching me for recreation.

So when it comes my time to leave here
I hope that my guardian angel is near.
Because I have one more job for him to do,
Poke a hole in the clouds and pull me through!!

Moods

When I am alone deep in a Dallas night,
I can feel your presence, warm and holding me tight.
It's just a night mood touching me.
Because you are home in bed, snug and cozy.

Your eyes are as blue as a summer sky.
I can hug you and just get high.
It's jut a mood from inside deep
I'd like to be with you...Asleep!

You work days, I work nights
And I wonder if this will ever be right?
When I am away, I miss you so.
But if I were there, would you want me to go?

Eyes

Why do your eyes talk to my soul?
Why is my heart under your control?
Why are my emotions on a sabbatical?
Why is loving you so impractical?

Your eyes are chocolate like a Hershey kiss
Your voice so full of promise and happiness
Your hug so strong and secure
Your love the kind that will endure.

I can close my eyes and smell you near
I can be with you and never fear.
I count your heartbeats with great care
I could share your love, accept your dare.

You could take my breath and run away.
You are the weather that makes my day.
You hold my life deep in your eyes,
And control my very being with
your special sighs!

Meltdown

I want to unbutton your shirt and make your skin ignite mine.
I want to touch your hair and absorb its' shine.
I want to make you so warm the color in your eyes will melt
And run all over me with a hot I've never felt.

I want your heartbeat to be the only sound.
I want to hear and feel it like sense-around.
I want your cologne to make me high.
I want your love to saturate me like a rainy sky!

I want my loving to create a passion you can't control.
A love that infiltrates to your very soul.
I want my love to burn in your mind, like a candle's flame,
I want to say your name and know you came!!

Touching Base

Did you ever need to touch the wall?
Or find a friend who was tall?
To tell someone special what you feel
And know the feedback would be real.

Home base is sometimes hard to find.
And umpires are very seldom kind.
Moon beams are fun to chase
But often take you to a scary place!

I look at you and wonder why
Someone loved you then said, "Good-bye."
That love must have really hurt
Cause warm tears wet your shirt.

A friend is someone very near
Who knows that hurt, but doesn't fear.
Because deep inside, they also know
That hurt will continue till you let it go!

A Fable

If I were little Miss Muffet
I would not sit on my tuffet.
I would put down the curds and whey
And come with you to share your day.

If we were there when Humpty took his great fall
We could super glue him and make him tall.
You and I, Jack and Jill
Could double date up the hill.

If I were Cinderella, I'd risk my midnight curfew
Just to leave you my glass shoe.
Because Prince Charming wasn't that dashing
And like Cinderella, I love party crashing.

If I'm not quite your cup of tea
Don't be sad, you're still you and I'm still me.
You took a chance and made a friend,
Life goes on, when fables end.

For Someone Quiet

I'd like to chart a journey through your mind
Untangle the mystery I'm sure I would find.
Seek the origin of your special smile
Sunbathe in the warmth of your eyes for awhile.

Marvel at the happiness that you store
And doubt anyone could convey love more.
You're sensitive, warm yet very unique
For your eyes say things you never speak.

About knowing you, I can't say I do.
No one knows the sky, yet we share the blue.
Besides a name is but a mere sound
Something to identify you in the lost and found.

DR. "K"

A strong, tall medicine man
Touching hearts, souls, and aging hands.
A man of caring with eyes of brown
Walking where death and sadness abound.

But look deeper into this special man.
Who comforts him, who holds his hand?
I see him smile, I hear him joke
But is his life complete or is it broke?

Things are said, feelings get hurt.
He is made of clay, treated like common dirt.
His dedication mistaken for greed
His love for mankind turned into need.

Maybe I can't see for wanting to
But I think your intentions are true.
So I will go on believing in you but wonder why
You can't find a cure before I have to die?

The Legend of North Tower

Once upon a time as legends begin
Comes a story of a tower in Dallas East end.
A dungeon with cells like long ago
A place of detention where criminals go.

I traveled from Irving to this place
A stranger, alone, the new face.
Within I encountered Sgts, Inmates, and SRT'S
Workers and inmates all with different needs.

Being medical, I eased their pain.
Tended wounds, dealt with psyche stress and strain,
The inmates as a rule were friendly and kind
I tried to be honest, fair, and sometimes blind.

But there are moments I choose to savor.
A smile, a touch, someone in need of a favor.
One Sgt. I depended on when things went bad,
One Sgt. who made me smile when I was sad.

A special SRT, in need of a back,
An officer's love of suckers to stay on track.
There are officer's, Deputy's and SRT'S galore
That I came to respect, work with and adore.

Now I have to walk away
Leave my friends alone to play.
But wherever life's road may take me
The love in North Tower will remain my special memory!

Wind

You are like weather, subject to sudden change.
Thus, my moods, I try to rearrange.
Wind never picks a certain course
Ever changing like a spirited horse.

Once in a while, our feelings collide!
But that doesn't mean choose up sides.
If we always thought the same
Life and love would be a boring game.

So when a storm warning is in the sky
Stay calm, cool and it will pass by.
Just because feelings sometimes get hot,
It doesn't mean, "I love you not."

Animation

Snow-white ask, "Cinderella, where is he?"
That knight in shining armor who said he loved me.
He spoke of friendship and noble deeds
But he is gone, with all his answered needs.

Lancelot laughed to Prince Charming
"Are we not good at being disarming?"
"We charmed those ladies, and rode away
I'll venture they are not in love with us today."

While not far away on a beautiful hill
Jack was declaring his love to Jill.
And snuggling close in the forest near
Robin Hood confessing, "Marian, you are so dear."

Is true love alive only in myths and books,
Is Peter Pan actually looking for Captain Hooks.
Did knights really slay Dragons that fly
Or was Superman just really an ordinary guy?

I want to eat at King Arthur's round table
And later create my very own fable.
I want a man gifted with romance
Who can steal my heart with only a glance.

Go to his castle and snuggle by the fire,
Create for him his heart's desire.
Read him a story about wizard's and kings
So he will feel the magic true love brings.

Dawn Hartley

Anniversary, St. Patrick's Day

You are the love song that I hear
Your eyes are the magic that keeps me near.
Your love is the happiness that I see
You, alone mean the world to me.

You're the morning that starts my day,
You're the rainbow, and rain that comes my way.
You're the reason for a blue sky.
You're the answer to the question why.

You're a million balloons, each a different hue,
Your love making makes it beautiful loving you.
You're all the things a "Silly Rabbit" should be.
You're happiness, love, simple, and free!

L. A. Freeway

While driving along in my Mac truck
Who else did I spy but Friar Tuck,
Thumbing a ride to his forest green.
God, was he lost in this automated scene.

I pulled my truck to a screeching stop
And ask him kindly, "Do you need a ride, pop?"
The words he spoke were very strange.
Like "Where goest thou on this concrete range?"

I answered him, "Wherever thou wants to goest."
He replied simply, "My sir, to Sherwood Forest."
So he got in and we were on our way
To Sherwood Forest via the L. A. freeway!

A little way down the road we passed this guy
Dressed in green with a long bow held up high.
"Stop there, sir, it's Robin Hood I see
Trying to find the forest just like me."

So we stopped to give him a ride,
When this squad car pulled along side.
He must have thought, what a strange crew.
A Mac truck driver, Friar Tuck and Robin Hood too.

"O.K. men what's this all about?"
I knew I was in trouble, no doubt.
Why did I not know this was not a good plan
Next came the handcuffs on my hand.

Dawn Hartley

Now I am sitting in jail wondering why
I didn't just drive right on by.
This is an adventure with only one small flaw,
How do you explain Friar Tuck to an officer of the law?

Nights

The sky was an enigmatic shade of gray
Moving quietly like monks on their way to pray.
My thoughts envisioned a castle atop a mountain ridge
Enveloped by a frigid stone drawbridge.

In a room saturated with a roaring fireplace
A knight resides with despair and sadness his saving grace.
Envisioning a maiden with dragons to slay
A valiant champion to vanquish the dragon away.

Adorned with armor, a sword and a plan
Our knight rides forth to battle, beast against man.
His trusted steed, his mode of transportation
He ventures forth to the destination.

The lady awaits with undying devotion
For the knight she summons with heated emotion.
But very much to the knights surprise
The only danger was in the damsels eyes.

The passion he felt, he couldn't explain
Driven by the force that accompanied the rain,
The heat from her touch made his body warm.
They were saturated by love generated by the storm.

But upon awakening, the knight had disappeared
And the love they shared imaginary, as she feared.
She lay in the rain and whispered his name
But without her knight nothing was the same.

She returned behind the castle wall
Realizing love wasn't there at all.
"I love you "is just what knights say
Before they steal your soul and ride away.

People

Sometimes you take a trip inside your mind
Just to see who you can find.
Sometimes an old friend, sometimes a new
Some smile, some say, "I love you."

With some you shared a real good time.
With some you couldn't tell logic from rhyme.
Some were warm and liked to share.
Some were cold and just didn't care.

Like that big, brown tree in the park.
That scared us to death in the dark.
Just like some people and some places
Fill your memory like familiar faces.

Inside your mind is a magic key
That can take you where you long to be.
With that person who said, "I love you."
And loving him was all you had to do!

Dawn Hartley

Because It's April

An April shower can be chilly or warm.
Making love can be a moment or an entire storm.
You can be magic, liquid and free
Or stormy, rough, and uneven like a jagged sea.

Sometimes I understand the things you teach,
Sometimes I wonder who you are trying to reach.
At times your eyes sparkle and shine,
Though I often wonder if you see mine!

You're difficult like a thought I was trying to write.
Mysterious, elusive, and awfully quiet.
Times I want to hold you like a big, stuffed bear.
But you reject affection like I wasn't there.

Perhaps someday, I will understand.
Be very bold, take your hand.
Ask you something I want to know
And wait to see if you tell me, "No!"

Real Important Things

Domino hotels where no one lives.
Unhappy people too selfish to give.
Houses made of diamonds and hearts.
Empty park benches, in big beautiful parks.

People with problems too big to face
Lots of money spent on a loosing race.
Where is laughter and children with toys?
Where are the good times, kites, little boys?

There's the freeway jammed with cars.
Here's a bunch of people drinking in bars.
There is the police officers with order to keep.
Here's the supermarket where nothing is cheap.

Give me the park with sunshine and clean air.
The majestic mountain because God is there.
The beautiful rainbow with colors that shine.
The real important things that are hard to find!

My Love

You're the magic that enchants my day.
You're the one who takes my heart away.
You're the music to which I dance,
You're my passion....you're romance.

Your body, the only one I want to touch.
Your love, the only one that means so much.
Your heartbeat keeps me company at night.
Your arms hold me ever so tight.

My life, I want you to share.
My heart, that beats because you care.
My bed, a very sacred place
Where only you can occupy space.

Tony

With his eyes, he could not see.
Yet he was showing life to me.
With just a touch, he could say
More beautiful things than words convey.

He could describe a ship with great detail
Walk in the woods and follow the trail.
He could hear the traffic light turn green
Tell by his bark if the dog was mean.

He taught the children how to survive,
But most important, how to be alive.
The sunshines' warmth by its touch,
The sound of love which means so much.

Even now I remember his smile
And why life is so worth while.
The things he said with his hands,
Remember, it's your heart that truly understands.

November Tapestry

Angelic artist have painted the trees
And their work colors the breeze.
Falling softly to the ground,
Painted November all around.

A cool crispness has sharpened the air.
The smell of fireplaces is everywhere.
Children are excited about turkey day,
Because ole'Saint Nick isn't far away.

The house has a special warm glow.
As the clouds promise maybe snow.
And bed is a sacred, tumbled spot.
Morning feelings drift, get up or not?

I am thrilled to see summer end.
Sunshine now is a warm friend,
Someone to hug in the cool.
Play in the snow instead of the pool!

Exceptional Taste

A pear taste like sweet, bits of beach sand.
You taste like sunshine feels on my hand.
The shower water from your neck, I taste
The liquid syrup of a chocolate cherry baste.

A Hershey kiss taste like moon light
Your smile taste like a banana's first bite.
Your love taste like wine, warm and free
You are an exceptional taste bottled just for me!!

Dawn Hartley

Blessings for You

May you have sunshine to start your day.
And beautiful friends with happiness to say.
May you have snow to trim your Christmas tree
And my Fall colors be warm for you to see.

May dreams you dream always come true
And may you always be happy and seldom blue.
May your favorite football team always have good luck
And may you never have to drive a Mac truck!

May happiness for others be yours to give
And may you always have enduring memories to relive.
May each day of your life be filled with love,
And may you always be respected and well thought of.

These are wishes simple yet true
And most of all, may someone always love you.
And when your life must come to an end,
May you travel not alone, but with your best friend!!

Life-Force

You're a lighthouse on a stormy sea.
You're my life-force surrounding me.
You're a light post shining warm and bright
When I'm lost and alone deep in a black night.

You're my shadow on a bright, sunny day.
You're my beacon, guiding the way.
You're a heartbeat that summons me near,
You're my best friend, and oh so dear.

You're the person I look for when I'm upset.
You're my reality when I try and forget.
You're there to slay dragons of heartache and despair
You're with me when my world needs repair.

You're the wizard of oz when it's home I choose to go.
You're the snowman I made in the snow.
You're a shoulder to cry on, a hand to hold.
You're my knight in shining armor, always loving and bold!

A One of a Kind Tree

Oh, Christmas tree, how beautiful you are to me.
The spirit of Christmas is very plain to see,
Underneath the branches that you unfold.
The gift of loving is about to be told.

It's not all those gifts, expensive and new.
It's the children's dreams about to come true.
It's all the love and magic from January one.
It's that baby that was born, Gods' only Son.

It's the spirit of Santa Claus, not the toys.
The hard times, sadness, work and small joys.
It's that special kiss on a snowy day.
That heavenly star that showed the way.

It's children's eyes all bright with surprise
That uncontrolled energy they can't disguise.
That turkey you don't eat the rest of the year.
The wise men who knew no fear!

It's having you to love my whole life through.
It's diapers, sore throats, yes even the flu.
But most important it is the gift of love
Born in a stable from God up above!

Holiday Blahs

Thanksgiving, the holiday season begins.
Turkey with stuffing, children and friends.
Another holiday without you.
Does Christmas snow come in blue?

I crave your smile, and most of all your voice
Conversation or a bit of snuggling, your choice.
I long for my reflection in big, brown eyes
Hugs by a fire that never dies.

Mistletoe is no good for kissing
As half of me is missing.
What has happened to Christmas cheer?
It is captured here in this Christmas tear!

Time Missing You

I can get angry in a moment of time.
Chew your butt, with no reason or rhyme.
But that is just me, and you should know
If I didn't care, my feelings wouldn't show.

Sometimes I'm asleep in a deep, dark night
I can wake quickly, wondering are you all right?
I know you think I don't miss you
But that is a silly male point of view.

I realize you work too hard, too much
And you need lots of human touch.
Because your heart is under reconstruction
I'll try not to be an interruption.

So here is your very own apology.
Straight to you from me.
Someday when you need a hug or a friend
I'll be right here, cause in love, doesn't end.

What Color is Blue?

God sat down one beautiful day
And said, "I will show my love in a special way.
Thus, I will create a magic hue
And I shall call this color blue."

He took his magic brush and made a big sweep
And created blue in the ocean deep.
Then He said, "This color shall be my sky."
And He painted blue way up high.

So now God's color we can all share.
It's blue we feel in nice cool air.
Sometimes the color of your best friends eyes,
That is soft and warm whenever he cries.

Sometimes that snowflake that brushed your face
Or the unique smell of a fresh fireplace.
Maybe the feel of your favorite old tree,
Or the friend in the dark that said, "Hold onto me."

That chocolate ice cream that tasted so good,
After you ran as fast as you could.
It is all these things and many more.
It is happiness when you're home at your front door.

That funny laughter you sometimes hear,
Or the soft, loving nudge of the little deer.
The feel of sunshine that makes you warm,
Or just an afternoon rain storm.

Dawn Hartley

Thus, God created blue for us to touch.
To show He loves us so very much.
It is what you hear in a special way
When someone says, "I love you and I need you to stay!"

A Birthday Wish

What can I give you for your birthday?
It's so simple, I hesitate to say.
Just the sparkle in your warm eyes of brown
A trip to the circus to watch the clown.

Years and years of watching you smile.
A day in the park, blue jean style.
Just a hot-dog with chili and cheese,
A chance to bless you when you sneeze.

Time to spend in the rain holding your hand.
All the old rock and roll we can stand.
A chance to tell you things on my mind.
Two dips of chocolate ice cream, your favorite kind.

Dawn Hartley

Bed Time Story

Today I heard a story from someone very wise
Complete with big, soft bedroom eyes.
A real cute story about cookies and bears.
That made me wish I had someone to tuck in upstairs.

Then tonight when the storm blew out the light,
I wished my story teller were here to hold me tight.
It was really sneaky of a friend,
To tell a bedtime story and not tuck me in!

But if he were here, I wouldn't need a story to sleep.
Because he is much sexier and dreams can keep.
So the next time I get scared, I hope he is around,
Since he is the most unique story teller I have found.

Time Maze

Seems lately I'm like a rat in a maze
Nights have now become my days.
When sunshine comes, I search for sleep
Chasing dreams I can not keep.

Time with you is pieces and bits
A constant yearning that never quits.
Loving you is hurry and go.
Whatever happened to romance and slow?

Days off are treasures to savor
Straight from God, a special favor.
Give me five minutes solid with you
And I will make forever come true!

Dawn Hartley

Four Year Old Wisdom

Rocks are something to watch out for.
Knobs are made to open the door.
Night time was made so we could dream.
Napkins are friends for thirsty ice cream.

Mothers are made to say, "No."
Dads were made to play in the snow.
Big brothers were made for hugs after scraped knees.
Grandmothers were made to grow your favorite trees.

Puppies eat things that you don't like.
Rain puddles were made to wash your bike.
Cats were made so you could have kittens,
Snowmen were made so you could wear mittens.

Popcorn was made for hungry Christmas trees.
Flowers were made so butterflies can sneeze!
Wisdom is a concept quite unique
But love is what four year olds see and speak!

Picture Thoughts

You're a mystery, I don't have a clue.
You're a very sexy man, I could love you.
You're warm and sincere, I'm scared to get serious
You're cool and distant, I'm upset and furious!

You speak of me, I'm on your mind.
You ignore me, you must be blind.
You know me, I wrote about you.
You have feelings? I don't know what to do.

You're at work, I see you smile.
You do your job, I think about you awhile.
You talk to friends, I wonder how you kiss,
You go home, why am I thinking this?

Dawn Hartley

Senses

I have eyes to wink at you as you walk by,
I have passion to make you high.
I have hands to hold yours as we stroll in the park.
I have fingers to excite you in the dark.

I have ears to hear the sound of your voice
I have the right to say no by choice.
I have a tongue to caress your ears when it's cold.
I have arms to hug you when you are bold!

I have moments to share your every dream,
I am the stronger member of this team.
I have days to be colored with sunshine
I always want to be loving and kind.

The rest of my life is at your beck and call
But remember, I am not very tall.
I have but one wish to ask of you,
Never say, "I love you if it isn't true!

Folklore

On a sunny mountain plateau
Sits an old man with memories of long ago.
His skin is wrinkled, tan, long ebony hair,
With eyes that see what used to be there.

He looks like a phantom of the old west.
A bear claw necklace hanging softly on his chest.
Perhaps he roamed this mountain free
Before the calvary, you and me.

Maybe he was a wild, young brave
With lovely Indian maidens to save.
He probably hunted buffalo and deer too
And fished blue streams, he could see through.

But now he just sits and watches the sun
Thinking of these times gone and days of fun.
The many buffalo roam free no more.
His teepee replaced by a reservation door.

That lovely maiden had since grown old.
With the calvary gone, no reason to be bold.
The young ones no longer hunger for his tales
Because there are no more wagon train trails.

He turns to look as we sit down.
But I doubt he knows we are around.
For as I look into his dark brown eyes,
I see the past for which his heart cries.

Seattle

A very, very special place
Where beautiful rain caresses your face.
Texas is hot and miles and miles away
But here we are together yet apart
I can hear your voice, but can't touch
your heart

How could I say good-bye to a
dream come true
How many ways can I miss you?
Why wasn't yes easier to say?
Why do special people always fly away?

I miss you even when I sleep
Why aren't heartbeats something
one can keep?
Why is it, hungry doesn't exist?
Lonely is never getting kissed!!

I don't get to see you smile
Pull off your shirt and stay awhile
Look at me with those big eyes of brown
Or turn my world upside down.

Well, now there is nothing I can do
Except miss you and be blue.
Hope that someday you will see
You can't be you without me!!!

Did I Tell You?

Did you know I would like to be
Your shirt, so you could wear me?
Did you know I'd like to be a clown?
So that I would never see you frown.

Did you know, I get lost in your eyes?
You are my star in midnight skies.
Did you know I'd break the law with
sheer delight?
Just to hear you read me my rights.

Did you know you're truly a gorgeous guy?
That being with you makes me high.
Did you know your touch makes my heartbeat race?
And all that I love is there
in your face.

Did you know that when I'm alone at night
I pray to God that you will be all right?
Did you know where ever you go,
Whatever you do
I will forever be missing
And loving you.

Dawn Hartley

Being There

Being there is more than merely occupying space
It is an exchange of thoughts from fingertip to face.
Touching someone is more than just reaching out
It is a force of touch that destroys doubt.

Caring is more than showing emotion.
It is a deep feeling resulting in an emotional explosion.
Talking is more than just speaking of words
It is words than are felt and heard.

Hugging is more than just embracing someone.
It is creating a warmth equal to summer sun.
Loving someone is more than just being there
It is the assurance of equality in the ability to care.

When I Hear Lance

When you talk about your French horn
All the anger in your voice disappears.
When you explain the notes and beats
I am no longer the enemy.

When you select the piece you are about to play
And place it gently on the music stand
I don't hear you screaming at me.

When you start to blow your horn,
I look to see your foot tapping lightly.
Suddenly I am just Mom,
Listening to all the beautiful music!

Dawn Hartley

Bridge to Tomorrow

I drove the streets of my hometown
As the falling rain slowly came down,
Like a squad of soldiers descending a ridge.
In my life, I was crossing an important bridge.

I would soon leave this place I grew up in
Travel away leaving my childhood, my family, a special friend.
The schools of learning where magic grew
From one plus one to two plus two.

The jobs that I had worked, the special secret places
Where memories lived on familiar faces.

In my mind, I knew I had to go
But the ghost of times passed said, "No."
As I stood in the cemetery getting wet
I cried and talked to my friend I'd never forget.

But if he were here, I knew he would say,
"Go on, I 'll never be very far away."
So as I watched the lights of the city fade into black
I knew no matter where life lead me,
I could always come back.

A Michael By Any Other Name

Today I thought about someone warm
With whom I shared many a rain storm.
His arms were strong, his thoughts kind.
His main concern only wishes of mine.

His eyes were big, soft and blue,
Beautiful windows I could look through.
He seldom laughed, but his smile was sincere.
He once tried to save one of my tears!

An Angel came to claim him the other day,
But even now he doesn't seem far away.
Whenever my world turns nasty and blue
I can hear him say, "That's O.K., I love you."

Dreams

It is raining out and I miss you.
I realize that most of my dreams
aren't going to come true.
I heard the dispatcher giving directions
Do they give assignments in heaven
after resurrection?

I miss touching you in the dark
Halloween and October in the park.
The warmth of your breath on my neck.
But your voice saying "I love you,"
I will never forget.

Your job now, is to look after me.
You can travel with the rain
Because you are free.

I know that you are out
Riding in a patrol squad
And then trying to explain
Your whereabouts to God.

Loosing A Soulmate

You left without my permission
or a simple good-bye.
I kissed your nose to remind you.
Now, memories are warm touches
in my mind,
We always said, "See you out there!"

I see you in squad cars, uniform.
My shower without your clothes.
I hear your laughter in the halls at work.
I kiss you in my dreams,
And actually hate to wake up!

I smell you in the car, your shirts.
I followed a stranger in the grocery store.
You were my Christmas everyday,
Death and I will never be friends!

Dawn Hartley

Unique Components

You're like a favorite old book, worn and wise
You are like a detective, always in disguise.
You are strong and tall as my favorite tree
You are someone special to me.

You're moody and colorful like a rainbow.
You're gifted as an actor in a show.
Your smile is as contagious as a happy clown.
You generate excitement like a touchdown!

You're refreshing like a summer storm.
Your personality and your hugs, always warm.
You're deep and sentimental like my favorite tune
You create romance like the glow of the full moon.

You are the embodiment of what a friend should be.
Your ideas unique, original and so important to me.
You are a dream that just came true,
In case you are wondering, this poem is about you!!

Just Because

Guess I'll learn skies aren't always blue
And people's feelings aren't always true.
Only one thing can make a bad time end.
And that is a special, close warm friend.

Someone to tell a little boy, why.
Someone to teach a teenager it's not cool to die.
Make love in a summer rain storm,
Stay very near and keep me warm.

Someone to buy balloons in the park,
And keep the sadness out of the dark.
Hug me close and sometimes say,
"I love you, please don't go away."

Quality Time

I'd like to be in the forest like Robin Hood.
Spending the day carving your name in wood.
I'd like to live in Camelot, like Lancelot
Polishing the armor, I know you have got.

Live on a desert island with you.
And get lost in the ocean blue.
Have your heartbeats to start my day.
Make love until the night changed to morning gray.

I'd like to be there to turn off the light
Snuggle close to you all through out the night.
Go with you when you leave for work.
Make certain you never get hurt.

I'd be honest, warm and kind
The best love you could hope to find.
And just in case you never knew
I don't want part, I want all of you!

Remembering

I remember watching the beautiful snow fall.
Being thankful that you were tall.
I remember our favorite love song
And knowing our love was strong.

I remember laying almost on top of you
Watching the sky go from black to blue.
Sharing your shower in my clothes.
Laughing about shaving cream on my nose.

I remember making Angels in the snow
And hugging you tight, afraid to let go.
I remember ice forts and snowball fights.
Warm fires and love-filled nights.

I remember touching you and big brown eyes,
Making love with you under Colorado skies.
I remember the Chaplain with his phone call
Now, I don't want to remember your death at all.

Wishes And Stuff

Did you ever want to kiss Santa's nose?
Or be a beautiful ballerina standing on her
toes?
Did you ever want to hug a big black bear?
Or slide down the banister on the stairs?

Did you ever want to catch a Phil Sims pass?
Or run through the sprinkler on the grass?
Did you ever want to be Harrison Ford's
co-star?
Or be in a western fight in a bar?

Did you ever want to write Neil Diamond
a song?
Or tell the third base umpire that he was wrong?
Did you ever count the drums in a street band?
Or wish ice cream wouldn't drip onto your hand?

I guess that I have wished these one and all.
And even wished I were tall.
But most of all I would like to know
Where do all my wishes go?

Photographs

Lightning photographed the evening sky
As thunder pounded close by.
We listened quietly to the rains musical patter
Realizing why touching can make love matter.

We watched the silky, shimmering sheets
As they dressed the cars, and washed down
the streets.
We lay enfolded in the magic, wet sound
Soon love and rain were all around.

The lightning continued its rapid course
Like a young, frightened, spirited horse.
The thunder talked in loud tones,
That shook our house like skeleton's bones.

Before long it will be Halloween
Witches, ghost, goblins and pumpkin scenes.
Children out to trick or treat
Creating fun which makes living so neat.

Presence of Mind

I can hear your voice and smell you near.
I can be lost, but with you my
destination becomes clear.
I hug you and want to go home.
Stay with only you and never roam.

I'd like to be trapped with you in a
raging, rainstorm.
Lick the raindrops off your neck while
they are still warm.
Listen to you breathe while you sleep,
Be the dream you'd like to keep.

I look into your eyes and wonder why
Someone hasn't captured such
a special guy.
Because if ever I got the chance
I'd fill your nights with non-stop romance.

I'd keep you near both day and night
Never ever let you out of my sight.
I'd try to make all your dreams come true.
Because I'm very much in love with you.

Once Upon a Dallas Night

At Parkland, once upon a cold December day
The spirit of Christmas arrived a most unique way.
Guided and proclaimed not by a star
But by blue and red lights that could be seen afar.

The mode of travel was not a small donkey you see
T'was a police car, a moving vehicle activated by a key.
The young officer filled with accomplishment
and great joy,
Had just delivered a bouncing baby girl and baby boy!

Not just one mother would bring us Christmas cheer
For labor and delivery was brimming with mothers
all very near,
To delivering babies by the score
Until delivery nursery could hold no more!

God summoned his favorite Guardian Angel and said
"Go and see if my Christmas story is being read."
Thus, the message he took back to his Master up above
"Yes, Lord, your babies are bringing
the world Christmas love."

"And upon my journey returning tonight
I beheld a most delightful sight.
An old man with eight tiny reindeer pulling a sleigh
Who shouted, "Merry Christmas" and flew away.!"

Chances

I'm going to take a stab in the dark
To explain your importance from my heart.
Your smile has an attraction of its very own
Your eyes the color of a solid, jade stone.

Your very presence denotes character and pride
Your words leave your mouth and touch me
deep inside.
Every location I share with you is a special place
A moment in time when a smile visits your face.

It's not fair I must share you
With a job, people and work to do.
I hate to think of you far away
Or you alone when night becomes a new day.

I come to you when I crave a hug.
Because in your arms I'm safe and snug.
I'd walk the high wire in the circus with care
Because if I fell, you would be there.

Paramount Revisited

Today I went to an old familiar place,
Sat quietly in the abundant space.
Looked at the screen, the stage, and rows
of empty seats,
Enjoying the calm, away from the noisy
busy streets.

It's just an old theater and my friend
Where I laughed, cried and spent days
without end.
It is built like a castle of long ago
Where you might expect Shakespeare to show.

The walls are majestic, beautiful carved stone.
The ceiling has stars when the lights are on.
As kids we joked about the ghost that lived here.
And as time goes by, he becomes more dear.

We named him Quentin, not a strange name.
We imagined him dark and dashing,
A pirate, with terror his claim to fame.
He lived way up high in the third balcony.
Sometimes, I felt him looking at me.

When I get a chance, I stop in to see,
Friends, wondering where Quentin might be.
As I leave and close the door,
I stop to thank Quentin for the visit once more.

Taste

Thirsty, like for the very first bite of
fresh fallen snow.
Cool, refreshing, like you I know.
Alone, cold and wet in a summer storm
Holding you, safe, snug and oh so warm.

Liquid sunshine stored in a jar
Pour you out, there you are!
Deep in your eyes a message so clear.
Your eyelashes lick my cheeks you are so near.

Wet, like a long swim in a clear sea.
Watching your heartbeat touching me.
My name on your lips, special indeed,
Scary, how you answer all of my needs.

Tired, like working long, deep nights.
Relaxing, watching the flight of high
flying kites.
Colorful like the multiple rainbow hues
Sharing all the many different moods that
compose you.

Detail Work

Tiny little hands reaching out to me
Searching little eyes hoping to see
Someone warm to touch, to hold
that little hand
To hug, to secure, to understand.

A rapid little heartbeat racing wild.
An infant on the way to becoming a child.
A tiny little creature from a secret place
With fingerprints, identity, a unique face.

Eyes of brown or mystic blue
Created by the uniting of two
With only a touch I have to convey
A feeling of security, just for today.

But what does this world offer this new being?
Crime, hunger, HIV, and drug dealing.
A mom and dad who must work to survive
Teens who learn to drink and drive.

If he could talk what would he say?
Why am I here, do I have to stay?
Where is my mom, will I grow tall?
Or will I have anyone at all?

Saints

Special people with special ways.
Sent by angels to brighten your days.
To guide, to listen, to understand.
To steady you, to hold your hand.

To face the odds, no matter the cost.
To be with you till the battle is won or lost.
To suffer your anger, share your smiles.
To follow faithfully for miles and miles.

To work in sunshine, be warm in snow.
To accompany you where you must go.
To agree when you're right, counsel when you are wrong.
To hold you when you are weak, to make you strong.

Through all your life your friend is there.
Stating in word and deed, I truly care.
Loving you with all my heart
With the belief, we will never part.

Reality Check

I thought love would wear forest green
and have big, brown eyes.
But he wears tennis shoes and has
Gorgeous thighs!
I saw love as cleaver and dear.
But he is so real and most sincere.

You're so much better than Lancelot
or Robin Hood
Because you are loving, honest, and
exceptionally good.
When I am scared, alone and in the dark
I can say your name and touch your heart.

There's magic in your voice and the
things you say.
Makes me wish I wasn't so far away.
I would do anything to make you see
How very important it is that you love me!

So Maid Marion has Robin Hood and
the forest stream.
I have you awake and even in my dreams.
Because when I want to make your
heartbeat fast.
All I have to do is just hug you and ask.

Musketeers Times Two

Touring daily through SMA
Cummings and Hartley make their way.
Floor by floor, cell to cell
One for security, one to see all are well.

Bound together Musketeers times two
Doing their jobs as partners must do.
With paper work galore and pills to pass
Laughing and talking, making time go fast.

A charming personality and big, brown eyes.
With Cummings, Hartley is just one of the guys.
Sharing their thoughts about jail and stuff
Especially how Gladiator was just too tough.

Bound together by camaraderie
This kind of friendship will always be.
But someday when life takes them
far apart.
Memories of duty in Dawson will warm their hearts!

A Sgt. In Need

Just a Sgt. with lots to do.
But are your dreams really coming true?
Two beautiful, little smiling girls
Torn between two grown-up worlds.

Alone in a city, big and bright.
Home drinking with friends at night.
Knowing tomorrow is just another work day.
Wishing lonely would go away.

Big, warm Hershey brown eyes
Filled with feelings you can't disguise.
Friends, people who really see inside
All the pain we try to hide.

Hugs are magic that makes us warm
And take away that emotional storm.
With a touch, a mere magic potion
Created to keep your heart in motion.

Love is just a moment away
Look harder for a love who will stay
To make your nights special and new
Someone to share your dreams with you.

A Rookie Cop

A Jafr is someone quite unique
An F.T.O. someone you meet.
The Sgt. responsible for what you do.
The Chief, someone who can keep or terminate you.

Under the microscope from day one.
Go to the firing range, learn the shotgun.
Love your handgun, learn to field strip
Drive the squad, the ultimate trip!

Talk on the radio, check in and out.
If you forget, dispatch will turn you about.
Take your baton, ask a few questions,
Ask how to locate a street, get lots of suggestions.

Drive the freeway, "code" 110
Handcuff the suspect, book him in.
Search to make sure he has no gun
Or that arrest could be your last one!

Meet the public, treat them fair
Or they will report you because you were there.
Take information for your report
Get it finished, time is short.

Don't wreck out the squad.
Hold tight to the wheel, trust in God.
When things go bad, hope that your vest
Will hold up to the bad mans' best.

Pen on your badge, shine your shoes.
Do the work and pay your dues.
A "Jafr" survives and changes into
A police officer, a cop, a man in blue!

Dawn Hartley

The Art of Logic

Logic, a most unique grown-up concept
One to be understood and made to accept.
It's logical to avoid a confrontation
But only in an isolated situation.

But in matters of the heart
Logic becomes an abstract art.
That beautiful brown in your eyes
Is that logic in disguise?

The sound of your voice that makes me warm
Is that logic in some alien form?
The confidence you instill in me
That must be the logic of philosophy.

Logic just can't explain
The beauty of a summer rain
The many colors of a rainbow
Or who actually designed snow.

You can't apply logic to the question why.
Or logically explain why friends we love die.
Logic just can't explain or cover
Children with guns killing each other.

There is no logic to HIV, cancer or homicide
Or drunk drivers who take a ride
In a car with wheels of gold.
Or nursing homes just because we grow old.

Damsel in Distress

She's but a damsel in the castle keep
In search of a love magic and deep.
To the young officers, she's a rare surprise
But an older knight she seeks,
with big, bedroom eyes.

She possesses bravery and lots of sass
Style and grace, beauty and class.
But in a ruckus, could hold her own
She could warm a heart or turn it to stone.

She's a mystic creature with a burning desire
To share the older officer's home fire.
To create a love, he will always treasure
And fill his nights with gifts of pleasure.

She must do her duties in the castle
Guide the young officers, though they are a hassle.
Cast her spell on the older knight
And wait for him to hold her tight.

Dawn Hartley

Lt. On Guard

A special man with talent rare
Patrols a dungeon with great care
He guides his troops through deep nights.
While the nurse possessed, creates inmates fights!

He uses his smile as a magic potion
And keeps his Sgt.. leading with
effective motion.
His officers follow his every direction.
Because his orders are not to be questioned.

The nurse he feels is ruled by voodoo
As even he can't keep order true.
She's a sprite much like Tinker Bell
Who we all know gave Capt. Hook, hell.

So as the Lt. tries to keep the sprite in check
All the inmates make his work a wreck.
But the sprite knows the Lt. is kind
And loves his heart and blows his mind!!

Time well Spent

I'd like to pick a place and sit down with you.
Listen to your thought, your dreams, what makes you blue.
I'd like to know the secret behind those
bedroom eyes.
Why you choose to be a man in disguise.

I'd like to know if you like ice cream
If you've ever had a truly, scary dream.
I know you gave away your heart
But what was it that made you part?

Sometimes I look at you and wonder why
Someone could love you then tell you good-bye
But that special thing about being a friend
Is a love that never has to end.

Friends can exhibit a temper and often do
Though that same friend could never hurt you.
A friend can look at you and watch you
walk away
And cry to remember why you acted
that way.

A friend is someone you don't take to bed
Though it is O.K., as long as it's only
in your head.
A friend's heart lays carefully in your hand.
No matter what happens, that friend will understand.

Dawn Hartley

High School

High school gym
the band, the noise
him.

Cheerleader yells
test grades, the teacher
swell.

Classroom flirtations
Homework, books
situations.

Work, the drive-in
sodas, beer
friends.

Parties, prom, fun
King and his Queen
a son.

Viet Nam, war
soldiers and dying
Quote the raven
Nevermore!

A Man In Blue

How do I thank you for the magic you give
Or all my fantasies you make live?
How do I thank you for the romance in your touch
Or the way you love me so much?

I could tell you, you're such a sweet man
But would you really, truly understand
That your very existence means the world to me
And very close to you is where I want to be.

I love the way your hair shines in the sunlight.
And sharing your jacket on a cold, Dallas night.
That your heartbeat is a unique sound
And your hands, the warmest around!

Now that I have let this little secret out
You will be difficult to deal with, no doubt.
Above all things I want you to know
I will always, always love you so.

A Mother's Fantasy

Today I'm a captain sailing a big, blue sea,
Or maybe a forest ranger planting a little tree.
A police officer working undercover,
A secret agent with an enemy lover.

A skier gliding down a mountain of snow,
A beautiful actress attending a premier show.
Perhaps a model with exotic clothes to wear,
A nurse filled with tender, loving care.

Would it really be nice
To live a life of variety and spice?
It is fun to take a trip in my mind
But I have a life of a unique kind.

I have children with dreams to share
A special love who is always there.
A beautiful home that is safe and warm
Someone to share my snow storm!

Excitement, romance and glee, a neat fantasy.
God saved the best life for me.
I'm all these things made into one,
And a secret agent couldn't have such fun!

Anthony

You were a pest in third grade
I hated those silly faces you made.
But I began to realize as we grew
I have always just loved you.

In high school I played volleyball
And tried so hard not to notice
you at all.
But there you were at every game
Giving me support just the same.

You were on the phone when no
one else would call.
You even promised me you
would not grow tall.
But you did and went to Viet Nam
Promised you would come back
if you had to bomb.

I was scared to death every day
Because you had never been far away.
I talked to God and ask him why
My classmates had to die?

I remember when that plane touched down
I bought every balloon in town.
And hoped I wouldn't take flight
Before I could hug you tight.

I came back home to share ice cream
Confirm you were real, not a dream.
But then you told me you were sick
And life would pass very quick

Dawn Hartley

We made angels in the snow
Went to every midnight show.
Dressed like Hippies and wanted
to go
To Height Ashberry, where it was
we didn't know.

Once Upon A Knight

The armor reflected the sunlight like a giant shield,
As the phalanx of knights approached the
tournament field.
The little girl watched quietly as the giant mounts
passed by
Bearing their riders with banners held high.

Then, for a moment he looked down
and saw
The little girl looking up at him
in awe.
The giant steed stopped in mid-stride
The proud knight now stood at her side.

The knight loosened the ribbon securing her hair
And tied it to his armor with great care.
Taking the small hand and bowing to
match her height
Smiled, and spoke," I will be your
champion this night."

He mounted the stallion, but turned to see
The small girl, her long hair blowing free.
The tournament that night was his to win
As his opponents fell time and again.

The little girl stood alone in the tournament ring
As her champion accepted his
trophy from the King.
The knight walked with great pride and determination
As the little girl watched with admiration.

Dawn Hartley

The knight placed the trophy in the little
girls hand.
In hope that she would understand
A knight needs a love to fight for and defend
And what greater a love, than a loyal
new friend.

All of You

I'd like to live in the forest
like Robin Hood
Spending the day carving your name
in the wood.
I'd like to live in Camelot like
Sir Lancelot
Polishing the armor, I know you've got.

Live on a desert island with you
And get lost in the ocean blue.
Have your breath to start my day
Make love until the night went away.

I'd like to be there to turn off
the light.
Snuggle close to you all
through the night
Go with you when you go to work
Make certain you never get hurt.

I'd be honest, warm and kind.
The best love you could hope to find.
And just in case you never knew
I don't want part, I want all of you.

Dawn Hartley

Back-up

Yes, a strange and puzzling term indeed.
Defined as friend, partner, help
in time of need.
You're all these terms and so much more
You're my companion through a magic door.

A leader, should I loose my way.
A rainbow, on a stormy day.
A clown, when the world makes me upset,
My favorite bookmaker when I want to bet!

My shoulder to lean on when I'm
not strong.
My counselor to advise when my feelings
are wrong.
My playmate when I decide to play in the park.
My back-up for when I am alone in the dark!

My reason to believe when nothing
seems logical
My Prince Charming making life magical.
My concerned listener with open ears.
My Priest who calms my deepest fears!

My champion, always protecting my domain
Slaying the dragons time and again.
But most important, I want you to be
My guy, who truly and honestly loves only me

Chris

He lives a cub day camp.
Down at the pool, where it's cool and damp.
But he's a rare kind of fish
In his heart lives a special wish.

With big, bedroom eyes of brown
He's skilled, talented and sometimes a clown.
But through all he does, comes a fantastic glow
That makes Chris fun to know.

His love for children, he can't hide.
Because it lives deep, deep, inside.
He teaches the kids to swim with care,
But if they need him, he is there.

When I look at Chris
I see kids and happiness.
I see balloons and ice cream
And a young man with an inner dream.

To make this world a better place
Where kids can grow and learn to face
All the problems that will come their way,
Like taking your first dive on a summer day.

Friendly Saints

Special people with special ways
Sent by angels to brighten your days.
To guide, to listen, to understand.
To stand with you and steady your hand.

To face the odds no matter the cost.
To be with you till the battle is won or lost.
To suffer your anger and share your smile.
To follow faithfully mile after mile.

To work in sunshine and be warm in snow.
To walk with you wherever you must go.
To agree when you are right, counsel when
you are wrong.
To hold you when you are weak,
help to make you strong.

Through all these times, a friend is there
Saying in word and deed, I care.
Loving you deeply, but with restraint,
Realizing you are but a man, not a Saint!

Halloween Treats

The moon is haunting, orange and bright
An eerie wind moves the clouds through
the night.
Witches, ghost, and goblins roam the streets,
Searching houses for apples and treats.

Deep in the night something wonderful is
about to occur
The siren cuts the air, red and blue
lights mingle and blur.
An expectant mother rides within
On the verge of delivery, moments left to spend.

Thus, one more to add to our human race
Delivered at Parkland, a busy place.
Another little ghost to haunt Halloween
An addition to this family, the cutest
little person they have seen.

Dawn Hartley

Pieces of Eight

If love could be valued like diamonds and gold
You would be too valuable to ever be sold.
If your warmth could be measured in a degree
You would be much warmer than
sunshine to me.

Pirate's often fought over
pieces of eight.
But more rare was a loyal mate
So if I ever sail the Seven Seas
I want you there to share the breeze.

Just like the snowflakes that fall so light
Summer rain storms and sunshine bright.
All the things I love so much
Most valued among them
is your special touch.

Jacky

When we met, you were very young and
didn't know
How very much I enjoyed watching
you grow.
But now you are a man older and wiser
And I am your much older advisor.

However, I learned to love you so.
But tried and tried to make you go.
I've taught you things that would
complete your life,
A good job, a home, a baby, and a wife.

Deep down inside somehow I've always known
When you were upset, hurt or just feeling alone.
It's like our emotions are somehow bound
One to the other strong and sound.

I've been with your through rain and shine
I've fussed at you, sometimes been unkind.
I've been there for you through good and bad
Tried to make you smile when you were sad.

I know someday when I go away
You will come to me and say
I can't go on if we're apart
So I will leave my love deep in your heart.

Just a little Book

Just a little book full of rhyme
Thoughts and feelings captured in time.
Here for you to read time and again.
Thoughts about you from inside
your friend.

Thoughts I could never say
When you look at me anyway.
But as you read them, they
touch you.
Something I can't do.

To trust is sometimes difficult indeed.
Most especially when it becomes a need.
Ask yourself, "Is love really real?"
Or just another people deal.

So just lay back and listen to Kenny G
Until you get really sleepy.
It is only ink and paper anyway
But your heart knows what the words
convey.

Making Love

Touching you is like Winter's first snow
Building the snowman you never
want to melt.
The first snowflake to touch your cheek
Angels in the snow who can almost speak.

Kissing you is like chocolate ice cream
On a hot, summer day
Running through the sprinkler on the grass
Holding onto you in the pool to stay warm
Feeling the thunder in a rain storm.

Loving you is like a sip of my favorite wine
Watching the firelight sparkle in your eyes.
Feeling your heartbeat inside me deep
Knowing I never want to go to sleep!!

Shape Shifting

Here's some poems to figure out
When you are already bored, no doubt.
A rookie cop in a shade of blue
To throw darts at, if you've nothing to do.

Someone who invades your time and space
And loves that smile upon your face.
You never know what to do around me
Cause you look at me but never see.

If I were a book, you'd put me down,
Go for a beer, or out on the town.
If I were on TV you'd change the channel
If I were your wall, you'd put up some panel.

So I'll stay a dream you don't have to keep
And only visit you when you are asleep.
For when you wake and search for me
I'll be there, you just won't see.

My RN 's Gift

There are so many things I'd like to say.
But let me start with, "Happy Birthday."
You've always been very, very special
to me.
And I hope this poem will help you see.

Here in the nursery is a special place
Because you make it warm with
your smile and grace.
You taught me things I thought
I'd never learn
You inspired my nursing, made my thirst
for knowledge burn.

And in those moments I would have
quit for a song
That look in your eyes told me
that would be wrong.
For these little babies truly need us so
And in your heart, you knew I could
never go!

God said, "To you I shall send a teacher
So listen, follow, and learn to be a seeker.
For the footsteps that guide you are
wise and kind.
The path you walk on is my Heavenly design."

Dawn Hartley

Ode to a Musketeer

Just to be walking in the forest and see
A musketeer riding his stallion right towards me.
What would I say to him to cease his ride,
Get down from his stallion and walk by my side?

Perhaps I'd smile and blush bright red
Or courtesy politely and bow my head.
Or walk as if I'd lost my way,
Hoping he'd stop, give directions and stay.

A man of honor, valor, and deep loyalty.
Charged with a dream, but guided by reality.
To share early mornings, and warm deep nights.
To value togetherness, but allow personal rights.

If you, Sir, be a musketeer,
Pick up this paper and keep it near.
For I will return with the morning sun
And we shall be one for all and all for one!

Out of Town

That stupid plane took you out of town
As I stood alone without you on the ground.
What a bummer to watch it fly
Knowing you couldn't hear me say bye.

The autumn air was suddenly cold
My knight in blue on a journey to be bold.
Stuck here with police cars and our park
Wishing this trip would end with the dark.

Two weeks, an eternity in time.
A punishment unfitting the crime.
I'm guilty only of loving you with all my heart
And being separated, a pain like being blown apart!

But time will pass, the plane will land.
I can see you smile, walk hand in hand.
Knowing this journey didn't change my best friend
And thanking God for you and the journeys' end.

Dawn Hartley

Parkland

Parkland is a famous place
Where humanities arrive and embrace.
With paramedics and police, dedicated all
Along with staff to answer each call.

Street people seeking shelter from the cold
Patients with HIV struggling to be bold.
Pregnant patients carrying a new life.
Emergency patients hurting from a bullet or a knife!

When a code is called, there is silence house wide
Knowing a patient might have died.
The battle for life is not always won.
God still decides the final outcome.

I've looked out your windows deep in the night.
And watched beautiful sunrises make it light.
Moment to moment. Person to person, life continues
And someone's story might make the Dallas Morning News.

Someday I know I will go away,
But all the moments gathered will stay
Locked in my memory until I recall
All the love and friendship in Parkland's halls.

High Stakes

Loving someone with your heart on the line
Hoping if you fail, you can pay the fine.
But should you win, his love prove strong.
Nothing you can do can make it wrong.

Hold him close, hug him tight.
Make his world beautiful and bright.
Love him deep, touch his heart.
Build a bond that can't be torn apart.

Feel his thoughts when he is away.
Touch his mind with words you say.
Let your heartbeats say his name
Feel his warmth like a hot flame.

He's in a world secret and far
Break the darkness, be his star.
Look at him, make him see
You must have him in order to be.

Dawn Hartley

Rainy Day Friend

Rain, rain come my way
So my friend will stop and play.
I look in the puddle and
who do I see?
A little girl who looks
just like me.
Whenever it rains, she comes
out to play
Oh, how I wish she'd
come everyday.

We splash in the water
and get all wet.
And at home, Mom
is upset.
The bath water is warm
and the bubbles white.
There is a smile on
Mom's face,
Everything is all right.

Into bed, prayers to say.
Thank you, God
for the rainy day.
The puddle of water
will soon be dry
But my friend will
return
With the next rainy sky!

Reese's Wisdom

You're a Robin Hood in the year 1988
On your leadership and guidance we wait.
Living within your friendship, love and words,
Absorbing all of you, like tiny little birds.

We depend on you to teach us to fly.
To tell the truth from a clever lie.
To help us control emotions too hot
to hold.
To love, to hug, but not be physically bold.

But our love for you is set apart.
To one, a confidant, a partner, protecting
his life and his heart.
To the other, a loving friend, a very, very
special being
Who guides my heart and must control my feelings

Rights

Thanksgiving filled with turkey and holiday
cheer
A time to remember the people and events
we hold dear.
The rights of life, liberty, and the pursuit
of happiness.
The rights of a mother and baby to
contentment and bliss.

A time to remember rights we take
for granted.
The seeds of freedom our forefathers'
planted.
The right to write or say
Our feelings on any given day.

So let us be truly thankful for God
up above
For families, friends, and those we love.
For Parkland and the job we do
Especially for all the babies who will
grow up to be thankful too!

Scarborough Faire

Outside the city, the year 2001
A British village stands in the morning sun.
A Camelot, complete with knights
who joust for the King and Queen
Creating an adventurous, royal scene.

There are shops of every kind,
Knights full of mischief, easy to find.
Roaming the village in search of
damsels in distress
Attired in their finery, looking their
alluring best.

There is Jacob's ladder, and games galore
Belly dancers spinning about the floor.
Sword swallowers, bagpipers, performers
all doing their best
To entertain citizens, visitors, all
their guest.

Merry Ole' England right here in
rural USA.
So bring your family out to play
The Knights will joust on horseback
while you cheer
Bring your camera to record the adventure
that you shared here.

Somewhere in Time

If it were in my power,
I'd set you free.
Return you to a time of loving me.
To that very special place
Where your love glowed on my face.

Where our hearts beat together
as one.
Though we were old, we loved
like young.
Our love was a bond, magic and unique
I could hear your voice,
we didn't speak.

Then a force began to grow
To turn our love as cold as snow.
I tried to scream, I tried to cry
You couldn't hear me, I watched
us die.

But someday our spirits will leave this place
The love will again glow on your face.
And the force that took your
love from mine
Cannot touch us somewhere in time.

Valentine Card

I thought I'd get you a card
But finding one expressing my
wishes was hard.
So I'll be Shakespeare and try
to capture your heart
Cupid would be luckier he's
got a dart.

I've been looking for someone just like you.
I made a wish, you made it come true.
You're funny, yet serious, warm and sincere
You're miles away, but your voice brings
you near.

You're like a walk on a rainy day
Exciting, refreshing, and enchanting in
a way.
My time with you is very special indeed,
Because you satisfy my every need.

So through this poem I hope you see
Flowers and candy are not that
unique to me.
I want to share Valentine day with you
one on one
Doing things friends do
loving and having fun.

Dawn Hartley

Wreck Scene

Driving the expressway with A.J.
Laughing, and talking about our day.
Traffic heavy, lots of brake lights
Crash!! rear-end collision, reality bites!

Looked at A.J., who had bounced about
Went to check the other driver out.
Driver O.K., her car a real disaster.
Very good thing we weren't going faster.

The rear-ender called her insurance without
hesitation.
Knowing wrecks to someone's rear
are bad situations.
Driving the expressway like the Daytona race,
But she was just trying to get home,
a very sacred place.

Me

I'm just like a windy day,
Can't make up my mind come what may.
I always see something I wish I had
Set a course, and the weather goes bad.

I'm like a ship on the open sea
Can't see the forest for the trees.
Pick a friend I would like to keep
Go too far, get in too deep.

I'm like a kid in a candy store,
Get just enough then find room for more.
Find the person to fill my life
Then realize I don't want to be a wife.

I'm just like a rain storm
Being cold when I should be warm.
Try to talk and reason things out
Then find my logic bulging with doubt.

When God made me, He spilled ink
on the plan
To add to the confusion, I use
my left hand.
In a world of right-handed glory
I don't play the lead in my own life story.

Even though I am not very tall
Life so far has been a royal ball.
Being Pisces, I'm kin to the whale
Who can't catch the wind without a sail.

Dawn Hartley

Memories

Today is your birthday, but you are not here.
You died last year.
But I am not going to miss you today,
I am going to summon you from far away.

I remember you laying by me in the grass
Talking about our day in class.
I remember you in the lake, teaching
me to swim
I remember you watching me play volleyball
in the gym.

I remember you teaching me to drive the car
I remember rescuing you in the bar.
I remember Viet Nam and missing you
at night.
I remember a welcome home flight.

I remember ice hockey on the lake
I remember ice skates don't have a brake.
I remember breaking my nose,
I remember you giving me your clothes.

I remember holding you and never wanting to let go.
I remember your eyes when you said, "No!"
I remember a firefighter graduation.
Then an arson inspector a different occupation.

I remember a smile that could melt snow.
I remember a hug that never let me go.
I remember your voice when you told me bye.
I remember I promised not to cry.

I remember every birthday you ever had.
I remember you never made me sad.
I remember your funeral and all the tears.
I will remember you, till the end of my years.

Dawn Hartley

Mom

The person who gave me a chance to be
The person who always listens to me.
The person I call when I'm upset
The person I know I shall never forget.

Someone with patience Jobe couldn't possess
Someone who said no, but more often yes.
Someone who came whenever it got dark
Someone who taught me to love with all my heart.

The person who took time to teach me to cook
The person who showed me the magic of reading a good book.
The person who taught me how to be wise
The person who taught me the beauty of rainy skies!

Someone who taught me how to care
Someone who got tired but was always there.
Someone who taught me how to love
My Mom, someone I'm very proud of.

I shall never forget your smile, the sound of
your voice,
I shall never forget you always gave me
a choice.
I shall never forget our talks, the time
we spent
Just being Mom and Daughter and how
very, very much it has meant.

A Summer Adventure

I've often thought I would like
to have wealth and fame
And just everyone would
know my name.
To have money perhaps to burn
Just spend and not be concerned

Then I go walking through the park
Kiss someone special in the dark.
Have a big snowball fight
Listen to crickets in moonlight.

These things are all free
Simple and plain just like me.
I'd find it hard to be rich
Not fun like wrestling you
in that muddy ditch.

Then go swimming without our clothes
Go barefoot and never powder
my nose.
Wear comfortable clothes like blue jeans
Eat fried green tomatoes
and red beans.

Cause money can't buy your love for me
Or be as fun as us up that tree
Jumping off into the lake
Meeting face to face,
that big Snake!!!

Dawn Hartley

The Spider

I sat quietly as the rain slid through
my hair
When I noticed the little spider
working there.
He was busy spinning his web
from limb to limb
Totally unaware a human
was watching him.

His every movement quite precise
His little legs looked like
a machinery device.
He worked as if he had
limited time
Like an invisible clock
would soon chime.

I remember a story
my grandmother told
She was American Indian
and never seemed old.
If you watch a spider
build his lair
Don't destroy it
for your future is there.

Suddenly the little spider
noticed me.
Stopped his work and
waited to see
At that moment I saw
something in my future
change
And I began to feel very strange.

I interrupted a moment in time
I heard that invisible clock
chime.
I now understand that missing part
Why you died and took my heart.

Dawn Hartley

Things I Love Most

I love little puppies, with big loving eyes.
Deep purple hues, forest green and rainy skies.
Smiles on people, guys in tight pants
You and your I love you glance.

I love the crunch of fresh fallen snow
The inquiring mind of a child who wants to know
Why leaves turn brown in the fall?
You, because you are strong, handsome and tall.

I love early morning sounds
When people hurry downtown.
Pine Christmas trees, police cars
With bright, spinning lights.
You, a heartbeat away on cold winter nights.

I love little babies cause they are sincere.
Little lambs, jersey cows and especially deer.
Popcorn, Hershey kisses and State Fair,
You when you want me to know you care.

I love American Indians and deep eyes of brown
Neil Diamond, the Beatles, Rod McKuen
and the rock sound.
Little boys, pro football, cheerleaders yells
You when you cast your magic spells.

I love horseback riding when it is cool
Going swimming nude in a motel pool.
Daisies, lemons, close friends and Coke,
You cause you tickle me with cute jokes.

I love the New York Yankees, the New
York Giants too
But most of all I love you.

123

124

ABOUT THE AUTHOR:

Dawn Hartley is merely the source these poems have
chosen to channel through. Ms. Hartley is a nurse by trade and a
mother of three by choice. Her poetry is a method used to
preserve special people, moments, and events that occur in life,
some happy, some tragic and some touched by fantasy.

www.ingramcontent.com/pod-product-compliance
Lightning Source LLC
Chambersburg PA
CDIIW031304060726
47590CB00003B/1055